GROW
By Design

A 60-day Devotional to Help Unlock Your God-given Potential

Jean Mpi

Published by KHARIS PUBLISHING, imprint of KHARIS MEDIA LLC.

Copyright © 2022 Jean Mpi

ISBN-13: 978-1-63746-139-6
ISBN-10: 1-63746-139-9

Library of Congress Control Number: 2022939812

All rights reserved. This book or parts thereof may not be reproduced in any form, stored in a retrieval system, or transmitted in any form by any means - electronic, mechanical, photocopy, recording, or otherwise - without prior written permission of the publisher, except as provided by United States of America copyright law.

All KHARIS PUBLISHING products are available at special quantity discounts for bulk purchase for sales promotions, premiums, fund-raising, and educational needs. For details, contact:

Kharis Media LLC
Tel: 1-479-599-8657
support@kharispublishing.com
www.kharispublishing.com

Dedication

This book is dedicated to Nyla and Naomi.

Table of Contents

Day 1
DARE TO DREAM 11

Day 2
A MASTERPIECE IN PROGRESS 13

Day 3
GO THE EXTRA MILE 15

Day 4
THE POWER OF MINDSET 17

Day 5
HIDDEN TREASURE 19

Day 6
MAKE THE MOST OF YOUR DAY 21

Day 7
KEEP MAKING PROGRESS 23

Day 8
CULTIVATE THE RIGHT HABITS 25

Day 9
STEP OUTSIDE YOUR COMFORT ZONE 27

Day 10
BELIEVE BIG 29

Day 11
THE EXCELLENCE FACTOR 31

Day 12
GROW THROUGH WHAT YOU GO THROUGH 33

Day 13
TRY AGAIN 35

Day 14
REDEEMING TIME 37

Day 15
YOUR WORDS IMPACT YOUR LIFE 39

Day 16
THE BEAUTY OF BEGINNINGS 41

Day 17
LEARN FROM FAILURE 43

Day 18
FROM SETBACK TO COMEBACK 45

Day 19
PURPOSE OVER PAYCHECK 47

Day 20
THE "I CAN DO" ATTITUDE 49

Day 21
GET MOTIVATED 51

Day 22
THE BEST IS YET TO COME 53

Day 23
BE A GOAL-GETTER 55

Day 24
DON'T BE LIMITED 57

Day 25
START TODAY 59

Day 26
DESIGNED WITH A PURPOSE 61

Day 27
MANAGE YOUR TALENTS 63

Day 28
AFFIRM YOUR FAITH 65

Day 29
YOU HAVE AN ADVANTAGE 67

Day 30
OVERCOMING GIANTS 69

Day 31
GOOD SUCCESS..71

Day 32
GET WISDOM 73

Day 33
TRAIN TO WIN..75

Day 34
FLOURISH THROUGH STORMS.....................77

Day 35
THE RIGHT ENVIRONMENT..........................79

Day 36
CHANGE THE WAY YOU THINK 81

Day 37
THE PROCESS OF PREPARATION................83

Day 38
EXPECT GOOD..85

Day 39
PARTNER WITH GOD.....................................87

Day 40
DISCOVER YOUR POTENTIAL......................89

Day 41
TAKE CARE OF YOUR BODY..........................91

Day 42
STAY CONNECTED TO GOD 93

Day 43
READ YOUR MANUAL....................................95

Day 44
EMPOWERING GRACE..................................97

Day 45
GROW UP IN ALL THINGS 99

Day 46
THE KEY TO BEING GREAT 101

Day 47

GUARD YOUR HEART 103

Day 48
LOVE IS THE KEY 105

Day 49
SEE THE BIGGER PICTURE 107

Day 50
EMBRACE THE NEW 109

Day 51
MEDITATE ON THE WORD 111

Day 52
SEE TREASURE IN OTHERS 113

Day 53
SHOW YOURSELF GRACE 115

Day 54
BE FRUITFUL 117

Day 55
WORK ON YOUR PERSONAL DEVELOPMENT 119

Day 56
OVERCOME FEAR 121

Day 57
BE FILLED WITH THE SPIRIT 123

Day 58
HAVE AN ATTITUDE OF GRATITUDE 125

Day 59
POSITIONED FOR SUCCESS 127

Day 60
YOU ARE LOVED 129

Bible Reference 131

About Kharis Publishing 133

Grow by Design

A 60- Day Devotional to Help Unlock Your God-given Potential

Day 1

DARE TO DREAM

> *"Now to Him who is able to [carry out His purpose and] do superabundantly more than all that we dare ask or think [infinitely beyond our greatest prayers, hopes, or dreams], according to His power that is at work within us."*
> **—Ephesians 3:20 (AMP)**

Dreams are pictures of the future that you dare to create in your mind. They don't necessarily take place when you are asleep, they can happen when your eyes are wide open.

Dreaming enables you to contemplate a greater reality than your eyes are able to see. God places a dream in your heart to show you a glimpse of your potential and to propel you in the direction of your destiny. Then, He works with you and through you to bring the dream to pass.

God is bigger than your greatest dreams and able to exceed them. So, don't allow your past experiences and present circumstances to limit your vision of the future. Don't let the disappointments of yesterday, water down your expectations for tomorrow.

> God is bigger than your greatest dreams and able to exceed them.

Joseph had big dreams which his brothers mocked and despised him for. However, when his dreams eventually came to pass, his family and an entire nation of people were saved from disaster.

The opinions of others should not stop you from pursuing your destiny. What is that dream that God has put in your heart? Do you have an idea to add value to the world? Perhaps you imagine yourself using your gifts to bless others? Somebody is relying on that dream becoming a reality.

You have the potential to dream big because you are created in the image of a mighty God. So, don't dream small dreams, dare to dream big!

Prayer/Affirmation

Dear Father, help me to dream and to imagine the good future that You have planned for me.

Further study

Ephesians 3:20 (AMP)
Philippians 2:13 (NIV)

Action

Write down a dream that God has given you, then keep it where you can be reminded of it often.

Day 2

A MASTERPIECE IN PROGRESS

"For we are God's masterpiece. He has created us anew in Christ Jesus, so we can do the good things he planned for us long ago."
—**Ephesians 2:10 (NLT)**

A "masterpiece" is defined as a work of outstanding skill or an example of excellence. It's a word often used to describe a person's greatest piece of work; one which showcases their ability and epitomizes their talents.

The "David" statue is considered to be a masterpiece of the artist Michelangelo. However, the statue wasn't always an impressive work of art. It started off as an unsightly slab of marble, which had been rejected by two previous sculptors before Michelangelo took on the challenge to finish it.

Today, millions of people visit "David" in Italy every year to marvel at Michelangelo's awesome sculpture. What was once a mess is now a masterpiece.

In his letter to the church at Ephesus, Paul reveals that we are God's masterpiece. It's amazing to think, that out of all of the wonders in the entire Universe, the Creator chose you to showcase His excellent workmanship.

> The Creator chose you to showcase His excellent workmanship.

God knows how to shape, mould, refine and enable you to become all that you were created to be. You may be a work in progress right now but God sees the finished masterpiece.

When you look at the back of a tapestry artwork, you see a tangled mess. But, when you turn it over and look at it from another angle; you see the glorious, intricate design that was being created all along. In the same way, God expertly weaves together all of the pieces of your life, even the messy parts, until He completes a beautiful work of art.

Prayer/Affirmation

I am a work in progress right now but God sees the finished masterpiece. He uses every season of my life to create a beautiful work of art.

Further study

Ecclesiastes 3:11 (NIV)
Philippians 1:6 (NIV)

Action

Take a moment today to dwell on the revelation that you are God's masterpiece.

Day 3

GO THE EXTRA MILE

"If anyone forces you to go one mile, go with them two miles."
—**Matthew 5:41 (NLT)**

Many people only put in the minimal amount of effort required to get something done. However, if you want to stand out from the crowd, you must be prepared to go the "extra mile" by exceeding expectations. You must be willing to go above and beyond the call of duty.

Jesus demonstrated this principle. He taught us, through His example to be generous with our gifts and share them with as many people as we can, as often as we have the opportunity to do so.

In a world where average is so common, you can make a difference by going the extra mile. When you do more than is required, it's not a wasted effort, instead, you're investing into your future where you will eventually reap a harvest.

You won't find much traffic on the extra mile because most people don't bother to take that route. If you want to live an extraordinary life, you can't take

> You can make a difference by going the extra mile.

the shortcuts, you must be willing to do what most people won't do.

Don't settle for average or to have an attitude of doing the bare minimum. God wants His children to do more, to give more and to demonstrate His abundant grace to the world around us.

Prayer/Affirmation

Father, help me to identify the areas of my life where I have been settling for average results. Give me the ability to go the extra mile from now on.

Further study

2 Corinthians 9:6 (NIV)
Proverbs 11:25 (NIV)

Action

Identify the areas of your life where you have been settling for average or less results. Make an effort to go the extra mile from today.

Day 4

THE POWER OF MINDSET

"But my servant Caleb thinks differently and follows me completely. So I will bring him into the land he has already seen."
—**Numbers 14:24 (NCV)**

The account of the children of Israel on the verge of the Promised Land, is a great example of the power of mindset.

God told the children of Israel that the Promised Land was theirs; all they had to do was go and take possession of it. So, Moses sent out twelve leaders; one from each of the tribes, to check out the land beforehand.

The leaders returned after 40 days to report back to Moses and the rest of the community. They gave a glowing report about the wonders that they had seen in the land. However, there was a major problem – the land was already occupied by "giants!"

Ten out of the twelve leaders gave a negative account of the prospect of going up against these "giants." Unfortunately, the majority of the people chose to adopt the same negative mindset

> God was pleased with Caleb for having a different mindset.

and unbelief. They were, therefore, afraid to enter the Promised Land.

Caleb was one of only two leaders to give a positive account. God was pleased with him for having a different mindset from the others. In the end, only Caleb and Joshua were able to enter the Promised Land, whilst the rest of the people perished in the wilderness. They missed out on the promise because their mindset stopped them from entering it. Today, people miss out on God's promises for the same reason.

If you want to take a hold of the future that God has destined, you must develop a mindset of faith like that of Caleb and Joshua, by believing that what God says is true. You must overcome the "giants" in your life to boldly step into your very own promised land.

Prayer/Affirmation

Father, help me to develop the right mindset so that I can step into all that you have destined for me.

Further study

Numbers 13:30-33 (NIV)
Romans 12:2 (NIV)

Action

Ask God to help you develop the right mindset to overcome any "giants" in your life.

Day 5

HIDDEN TREASURE

"The kingdom of heaven is like treasure hidden in a field. When a man found it, he hid it again, and then in his joy went and sold all he had and bought that field"
—**Matthew 13:44 (NIV)**

There was a story about a person who had unknowingly kept a valuable antique ornament in his home for many years. Instead of being put on display, the ornament had been used as a doorstop to prop open the living room door because the owner was completely ignorant of its true value.

One day, an auctioneer visited the home to value some other items which the owner was planning to sell. The auctioneer immediately recognized the ornament lying on the living room floor. It was in fact an ancient Chinese antique worth over a quarter of a million dollars! It was a treasure, yet for many years, it had been treated like trash.

When you use something for a purpose that it wasn't designed for, its value will go to waste. Everyone needs someone like the auctioneer; who can call out the treasure in another person and help them to discover their potential.

> Your true value is determined by God.

You are worth much more to God than any ancient antique. Thankfully, your true value is determined by Him, not by the ignorance of other people. When you discover who you really are and step into the fullness of your purpose, others will also benefit from the hidden treasure inside you.

Prayer/Affirmation

Father, help me to discover the treasure You have hidden inside me and in others.

Further study

Matthew 5:14-16 (NIV)
Matthew 13:44 (NIV)

Action

Think of one way you can help someone discover their potential.

Day 6

MAKE THE MOST OF YOUR DAY

"Teach us to realize the brevity of life, so that we may grow in wisdom."
—Psalm 90:12 (NLT)

It's not unusual to get to the end of the day and wonder where the time went. You can, however, make the most of each day by being more intentional with your time. Simple changes can lead to great results and developing better habits can lead to a better lifestyle.

Firstly, how you start the day can play an important factor in determining how the day goes. Try to wake up before the "busyness" of the day starts. You don't need an elaborate morning ritual; a few minutes spent on some simple practices will help set you up for a good day.

Aim to start each day with God through prayer, affirmations, devotion time or meditation. These are all great ways to prepare your heart, focus your mind and receive wisdom for the day ahead.

> Make the most of each day by being more intentional with your time.

Secondly, if your day is too busy, it can lead to an unproductive outcome. Try to plan ahead by preparing the night before or writing down the important tasks in a planner. Writing things down will help free your mind of clutter and allow you to organize your time more effectively. Research shows that you are more likely to get things done if you write them down. Be intentional but also prepare to be flexible with your plans.

Finally, don't feel under pressure by reports of people who wake up at 4am every morning and accomplish everything by 8am. It's not a very practical routine for most people! You must accept the fact that some days you will be more productive than others.

Give yourself the grace to make adjustments and do what works for you in each season of your life. Most importantly, ask God for the wisdom to help you make the most of each day.

Prayer/Affirmation

Father, help me to use my time well and remind me to start each day with You. Give me the wisdom to make the most of each day.

Further study

Proverbs 16:3 (NIV)
James 1:5 (NIV)

Action

Choose at least one morning practice, then do it consistently for the next 30 days.

Day 7

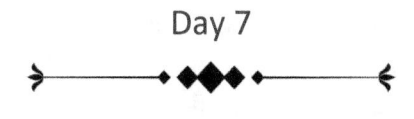

KEEP MAKING PROGRESS

"Then Isaac sowed in that land, and received in the same year an hundredfold: and the Lord blessed him. And the man waxed great, and went forward, and grew until he became very great:"
—**Genesis 26:12-13 (KJV)**

There are very few things more frustrating than not making progress in one or more areas of your life. That's because you were not designed to remain stagnant, you were designed to keep growing and to keep making progress.

The natural world always seems to strive towards its highest potential. A tree, for example, doesn't grow halfway then decide it's had enough! No, it uses all of the available nutrients to help it mature and grow as tall and healthy as possible. Life should be a journey of constant growth, learning and improvement.

There are some seasons when making progress may seem impossible. However, despite challenging circumstances, you can still keep moving forward.

Isaac lived through a difficult period of extreme famine. This means that there would have been a shortage of food caused

> Life should be a journey of constant growth, learning and improvement.

by a scarcity of crops. The land wasn't conducive to growing food, yet Isaac not only sowed in that land but in the same year, he reaped "an hundredfold" harvest! In spite of the circumstances, Isaac kept moving forward. He made progress and grew until he became very great.

True progress is not about comparing yourself with others; it's about moving steadily in the direction of God's unique plan for your life. The amount of progress you make externally is closely linked to your internal growth. You will soon notice that as you change, things around you will start to change. When you become better, everything you do will become better. Eventually, your progress will be obvious, visible and noticeable to those around you.

Like Isaac, the seeds you sow today will result in a multiplied harvest of results in the months and years to come.

Prayer/Affirmation

Father, help me to keep moving forward and to make steady progress in every area of my life.

Further study

Psalm 1:3 (NIV)
1 Timothy 4:15 (NIV)

Action

Identify at least one area of your life where you would like to see progress and take action towards making a change.

Day 8

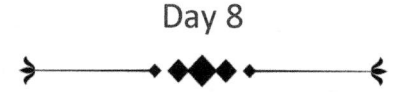

CULTIVATE THE RIGHT HABITS

"But the Holy Spirit produces this kind of fruit in our lives: love, joy, peace, patience, kindness, goodness, faithfulness, gentleness, and self-control. There is no law against these things!"
—**Galatians 5:22 (NIV)**

A habit is formed when you repeat a pattern consistently over a period of time until it becomes second nature. Good patterns don't happen by accident, they require patience and self-control, which are both fruit of the Spirit.

It takes roughly 60 days to form a new habit. So, even if you have unintentionally formed bad habits, you can intentionally change and replace them with better ones. This is possible with the help of the Holy Spirit working through you; helping you turn good intentions into good actions, good actions into good habits and good habits into a good lifestyle.

By spending your time doing the things you should do, you will have little time to do the things you shouldn't. By channeling your energy into cultivating good habits, you take your focus away from negative distractions.

> To live to your full potential you must build the right habits.

Good habits are necessary for good success. To live to your full potential, you must build the right habits into your life; such as prayer, studying the Bible, maintaining a healthy lifestyle and consistently engaging in activities that will help you grow.

Prayer/Affirmation

Father, help me to develop patience and self-control to replace any bad habits with good habits instead.

Further study

Psalm 1:2 (AMP)
1 Corinthians 9:25 (NIV)

Action

Ask God to help you identify any bad habits that you need to change.

Day 9

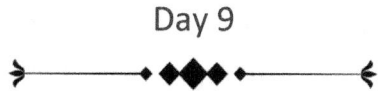

STEP OUTSIDE YOUR COMFORT ZONE

"The Lord had said to Abram, 'Go from your country, your people and your father's household to the land I will show you.'"
—**Genesis 12:1 (NIV)**

Your comfort zone, as the name suggests, is any place where you feel comfortable, familiar and unchallenged. It's also often the place where you experience minimal growth, development or progress. After a while, a comfort zone can become restricting and uninspiring.

Stepping out of your comfort zone involves stepping out in faith and taking some risks in pursuit of all that God has planned for you.

Many people stay in familiar surroundings because they fear the unknown. To step out of your comfort zone, you don't have to know all of the details of where you are going, you just need to be willing to take the first step of faith.

Abraham had to move out of his comfort zone and go away from his familiar surroundings before he was able to fulfil his purpose. At first, he didn't know where he was going but he trusted that

> Stepping out of your comfort zone involves stepping out in faith.

Grow by Design

God would lead him to the right place. With each step he took, more details were revealed to him. Generations of people around the world have been blessed because Abraham took that first step of faith.

If you want to grow, you have to be willing to be uncomfortable at times. Fear will try to paralyze you from going beyond what you are used to. Don't let the fear of uncertainty hold you back from what God has planned for you. Like Abraham, you must be willing to step outside your comfort zone by faith, to become the person that you are destined to be.

Prayer/Affirmation

I am stepping out of my comfort zone and into all that God has planned for me.

Further study

Genesis 12:3 (NIV)
Hebrews 11:8-9 (NIV)

Action

What "comfort zone" is God calling you out of? Decide today to take the first step of faith.

Day 10

BELIEVE BIG

*"What do you mean, 'If I can'?" Jesus asked.
"Anything is possible if a person believes."*
—Mark 9:23 (NLT)

The world around us mostly conditions us to be "realistic" or to "play it safe." This leads to so many people living small lives, way below their potential and far below God's plan for them.

When God wanted to inspire Abraham to believe for something big, He gave him a vision of the promise. He took Abraham outside and asked him to count the stars so that he could see how many descendants he would have. At the time, Abraham was childless, yet the night sky was filled with stars.

When Abraham realised that the stars were indeed countless, the magnitude of God's plan for his future began to dawn on him. Finally, he was able to believe for the fullness of the promise that was coming his way.

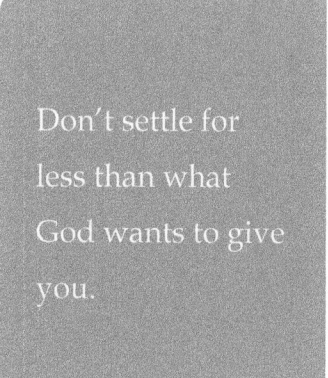

Don't settle for less than what God wants to give you.

Abraham and Sarah had been believing for one child but God wanted them to birth an entire nation. They had been believing for God to bless them but God wanted to bless generations of people through them!

Don't settle for less than what God wants to give you. The process of believing for big promises to come to pass in your life can be challenging, as it requires faith and patience. Don't let the confines of your current situation restrict you. Don't be conformed to the limited thinking of the world around you. Let God's Word renew your mind and inspire a bigger vision of the future to believe for.

Prayer/Affirmation

Father, help me to expand my vision and increase my faith so that I can believe that what You have planned for me is possible.

Further study

Genesis 15:5-6 (NIV)
Hebrews 6:12 (NIV)

Action

Ask God to give you a vision of your future to believe for.

Day 11

THE EXCELLENCE FACTOR

"Then this Daniel became distinguished above all the other high officials and satraps, because an excellent spirit was in him."
—Daniel 6:3 (ESV)

The excellence factor is something that will set you apart in the midst of mediocrity. Excellence is a quality that people admire because it's not common. It's displayed in the things that you do and how you do them. It can be seen in the way you present yourself and treat other people. It even comes across in your choice of words and how you speak.

The art of excellence is developed over time; it will cause you to stand out and become distinguished. You don't necessarily have to be the best to be excellent; you just need to do the best with whatever God has given you. Our homes, places of work and communities would be so much better if each individual worked with this attitude.

You must start by cultivating excellence from within, the kind that comes from a good moral character and a mindset shaped by God's Word. This will in turn overflow effortlessly into everything you do.

No matter what your background is or what your present reality

> Excellence is a quality that people admire because it's not common.

looks like, you can make a commitment to become excellent. There is no need to struggle or strive for perfection. As you work in partnership with the Holy Spirit, He will take you through a process of refinement and transformation. He will help you develop, improve and learn newer, better ways of doing things that will make you excel in any area of life.

The excellence factor was the reason why Daniel was promoted to a position of leadership in a foreign land. It was the thing that set Joseph apart and helped promote him from the prison to the palace. The excellence factor can do the same for you today. When you do ordinary things in extraordinary ways, you reflect the splendour of God to the world around you, for His glory.

Prayer/Affirmation

I make a commitment to become excellent and do excellent things for the glory of God.

Further study

Proverbs 22:29 (NKJV)
Philippians 4:8 (NIV)

Action

Think of at least one area of your life that you would like to become more excellent in. Ask God to show you how to achieve this.

Day 12

GROW THROUGH WHAT YOU GO THROUGH

"Good people will prosper like palm trees, and they will grow strong like the cedars of Lebanon."
—**Psalm 92:12 (NLT)**

The book of Psalms often draws analogies between the natural world and human behaviour or characteristics. The above scripture compares good people to cedar trees, which have played a vital role throughout history.

The majestic cedars grow in the mountainous regions of Lebanon and remain evergreen through the harsh, snowy winter seasons. Just like the cedar tree, you can grow and thrive through difficult seasons.

Firstly, as you navigate a challenging time in your life, remember that it won't last forever. Just like in nature, the winter seasons of life are preparing us to embrace the brighter seasons ahead. So, when you face your own dark winter, remember that it is only temporary.

If you are going through a season of disappointment, hold on because a new season of fulfilment will soon come. If you are going through a season of sadness or pain, take heart

> You can grow and thrive through difficult seasons.

because a new season of overflowing love and joy will break through. If you are going through a season of scarcity, don't give up because a new season of abundant harvest will eventually arrive.

Secondly, remember that difficult seasons do not define who you are. Joseph went through the pit and prison before he eventually made it to the palace. No matter what stage Joseph was in, God still blessed him there. Similarly, God's dreams, plans or promises for you remain the same despite the challenging times you go through.

Finally, remember that each season can teach us something which will help us thrive in the next. In the pit and prison, Joseph didn't realise that his character was being shaped and refined for his calling to the palace. As seasons come and go, God doesn't want you to remain the same. You can decide to keep growing and learning in spite of anything that comes your way.

Prayer/Affirmation

I believe that each season I go through is shaping me and preparing me for a purpose that God has planned for me.

Further study

Genesis 8:22 (NIV)
Romans 5:3-5 (NLT)

Action

Write down at least one helpful life lesson you have learnt in your current season.

Day 13

TRY AGAIN

"Master.. we worked hard all last night and didn't catch a thing. But if you say so, I'll let the nets down again."
—Luke 5:5 (NLT)

Most of us have ideas, dreams and goals. However, they don't always succeed in the way that we hope. After experiencing disappointment or discouragement, it can be difficult to pick yourself up, dust yourself off and try again.

If you have an idea, dream or goal which could add value to the world around you or improve the lives of others, don't give up just yet. The journey to success will help to develop you. Your idea may fail the first few times but the experience you gain can help you develop the qualities that you need to prepare you for when the right opportunity comes.

Simon Peter and some of the other disciples had been out fishing all night and had caught no fish. Then suddenly in the morning, Jesus appeared and asked them to try again. He told them to throw their net down, this time on the right side of the boat.

> The journey to success will help to develop you.

These disciples were experienced fishermen, they knew a lot about fishing, they had toiled all night, yet they had caught nothing. They would have been quite reluctant to try again. However, instead of complaining, Peter did as Jesus had instructed. This time, they caught a massive haul of fish, so big that their nets started to break and their boats almost sank from the weight of the catch!

Sometimes, all you need is for God to give you a new direction, instruction or wisdom that will help you solve the problem. That thing you've been working hard at, with little results, will suddenly become a success.

Keep going, don't give up just yet. Let your experiences develop you and prepare you for success ahead.

Prayer/Affirmation

Father, give me the courage, direction, instruction or wisdom to try again. This time, cause my efforts to be successful.

Further study

Psalm 90:17 (NLT)
James 1:5 (NIV)

Action

As you receive fresh instruction, direction or wisdom from God, give your dream or idea another try.

Day 14

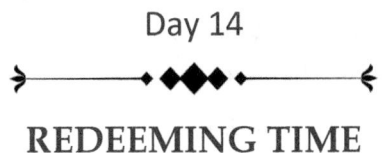

REDEEMING TIME

"..redeeming the time because the days are evil."
—**Ephesians 5:16 (NKJV)**

Time is a universal currency. No matter where you are in the world, time is the one thing that every person has the same access to.

Whether you're in New York or New Zealand, the United Kingdom or the United Arab Emirates; no matter your background, age or status, every person has 24 hours credited to their daily account.

The problem is that many people find themselves needing more time than is available. How often do you get to the end of the day, week, month or even year and wonder: "where did the time go"? If you don't learn to manage your time well, there are many things that will seek to steal it.

The word translated as "redeeming" in the opening scripture, means to rescue from loss; to recover or to reclaim something.

God, in His wisdom, determined that 24 hours is all that you need to accomplish His purpose for you each day. He has given you

> Every person has 24 hours credited to their daily account.

all the time you require to do the things He planned for you to do. Often, it's a lack of direction that's the issue not lack of time. So, how can you overcome this?

Well, you must be intentional about how you're spending your time so that you can get the most out of each day. Learn to budget your time effectively, like you would do with your finances. Spend it on the right things, invest it wisely and don't waste it on nonsense! Don't let precious time pass you by without doing all you can to steward it well.

Prayer/Affirmation

Father teach me to manage my time wisely so that I can do the things which You have planned for me to do.

Further study

Psalm 90:12 (NLT)
Ephesians 5:16 (AMP)

Action

Use a planner or notebook to help manage your time effectively.

Day 15

YOUR WORDS IMPACT YOUR LIFE

"Death and life are in the power of the tongue, and those who love it and indulge it will eat its fruit and bear the consequences of their words."
—**Proverbs 18:21 (AMP)**

The words you speak can have a significant impact on your life. The quality of your life today is largely a result of the words you have been speaking up until now, especially the things you say about yourself. If you consciously manage your words, then you can influence the direction of your life.

Think of your mouth as a tap; when you open it, what comes out is an overflow of what is stored inside your "heart tank." If you fill your heart up with the right things, then your mouth is more likely to release the right words.

Your words can impact your life by attracting either life or death. You may not be able to completely control everything that comes out of your mouth but you can choose to not use your words carelessly. You can put this into practice by intentionally affirming your faith.

When you speak out your fears, you begin to attract the manifestation of them into your

> Your words can impact your life by attracting either life or death.

life. When you speak out faith, then you begin to see the promises of God come to pass in your life. The effects might not show up right away but eventually, they will. You can choose to either speak life or death, to speak blessing or destruction.

God demonstrated, during the account of Creation in the Book of Genesis, that words have creative power. The physical world that we see is made up of and governed by the invisible world that we don't see. This is scientific fact and spiritual truth.

Likewise, you are made in God's image; therefore you have the power to create your own "world" by the words which you speak. Imagine that words are like the spiritual scaffolding which frames your future. How you use your words will help determine what kind of life you build. So, if you want to change the way your life is today, speak words to help reframe your tomorrow.

Prayer/Affirmation

I am speaking life-giving, faith-affirming words to move my life in the direction of my God-given destiny.

Further study

Proverbs 4:23 (NIV)
Hebrews 11:3 (NIV)

Action

When you wake up in the morning, speak blessings over your day ahead.

Day 16

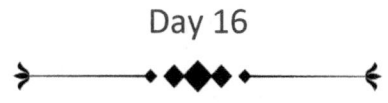

THE BEAUTY OF BEGINNINGS

"Do not despise these small beginnings, for the Lord rejoices to see the work begin.."
—**Zechariah 4:10 (NLT)**

Great things often spring from little beginnings. God designed the world so that practically everything starts out small before it becomes great. Small babies grow up to become powerful leaders. Tiny apple seeds blossom to become fruitful orchards. Little acorns flourish into mighty oak trees.

Perhaps you have an idea or dream but you don't know how to make it happen. You may not have all of the skills, experience or resources you need at the beginning. Start with the little you have to work with, mix it with faith and allow God to do the rest.

Be faithful and diligent with the responsibilities that you have now. Then, God will be able to entrust you with more. During small beginnings, He refines your character, proves your faithfulness and prepares you for your higher calling.

> Great things often spring from little beginnings.

The Bible is full of examples of people who started small then went on to fulfill great destinies. David started as a young shepherd boy and became a mighty king. Esther started as an orphan in a foreign land where she eventually became queen.

There is beauty in small beginnings. God is pleased when you start out in faith and He gives you the grace to grow into the fullness of your destiny. Remember, the journey to greatness starts with a small step of faith.

Prayer/Affirmation

Father, thank You for the beauty in beginnings. Help me to start out in faith and grow into all that you have called me to.

Further study

Zechariah 4: 6 (NIV)
Luke 16:10 (NIV)

Action

Don't be afraid to start with what you have now and watch God multiply it.

Day 17

LEARN FROM FAILURE

"Even if good people fall seven times, they will get back up."
—**Proverbs 24:16 (CEV)**

In life, the question is not whether you will experience failure, but rather how you will deal with failure when it comes. Real personal growth happens when we go through tough times and emerge from them better, stronger and wiser than we were before.

Failure is often difficult to accept, embarrassing to admit and challenging to navigate. However, when you change your perspective; you can see God use these situations to lead you to success.

Failure doesn't mean finality. Just because something didn't work out for you, that doesn't mean there is something wrong with you.

Sometimes when you fail at something, it's because it is leading you to something greater. The key is to learn from the failure and use it as a stepping stone to move forward. Some of the greatest inventions, discoveries and innovations were the result of mistakes or failed attempts.

> Learn from failure and use it as a stepping stone to move forward.

Be encouraged, there are some successes that you will never achieve unless you stumble, get back up and learn along the way.

Prayer/Affirmation

I am not defined by any failure; instead, I learn from it and use it as a stepping stone on my journey to success.

Further study

Jeremiah 29:11 (NIV)
Philippians 3:13 (NIV)

Action

Write down at least one lesson failure has taught you, that you can use on your journey to success.

Day 18

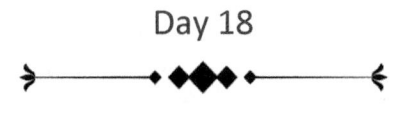

FROM SETBACK TO COMEBACK

"God has made me forget all my troubles... God has made me fruitful in this land of my grief."
—Genesis 41:51- 52 (NLT)

If you have experienced a setback in your life, that is not where your story ends. The Bible is full of examples of people who went from a disappointing season of setbacks to a glorious comeback.

Joseph suffered many years of setback when it looked as though his dreams would never come to pass. But when they did, his comeback was a great one. His turnaround was so dramatic that Joseph was able to forget all of the troubles he had endured. In an instant, God can restore to you more than you lost. He can bless you so much that you forget the troubles you went through.

Job was an extreme example of someone who suffered many setbacks. He lost nearly everything but thankfully, that Chapter wasn't the end of his story. Before the end of the book, there is an awesome turnaround. God gave Job twice as much back as he had lost. So much so, that his latter days were more blessed than his former.

> In an instant, God can restore to you more than you lost.

It looked as though it was all over for Jesus, after he suffered what seemed like a humiliating defeat on the cross. Little did His enemies know that the cross was just a setup for the resurrection and a prelude to the greatest comeback story of all time!

No matter what setbacks you might have experienced, your future can be more blessed than your past. God can use the trouble that you thought would finish you to strengthen you, develop you and help you become the person He created you to be. Often, what looks like a problem can actually be the very thing that propels you towards your destiny.

Prayer/Affirmation

Father, thank You for turning my setbacks into comebacks and making my future more blessed than my past.

Further study

Job 42:10 (NIV)
Ephesians 2:6 (NIV)

Action

Think of an amazing comeback story and let it inspire you with hope today.

Day 19

PURPOSE OVER PAYCHECK

"Work willingly at whatever you do, as though you were working for the Lord rather than for people."
—**Colossians 3:23 (NLT)**

There is a purpose behind the work that you do that goes beyond just getting a paycheck. Your work has the potential to change lives and impact other people positively. When you are motivated by this purpose, there is a greater sense of fulfilment that comes with doing your work.

You don't have to be in a church setting to do meaningful work or to serve others. God needs His people to work in every sphere of society so that He can bring His plans to pass there. He needs people in government, media, the corporate world, schools, the marketplace, hospitals and so on.

Around a third of your time will be spent at work, so it's not enough to simply go to work to earn money to pay your bills. Such a significant investment of your time has to serve a higher purpose.

> There is a purpose behind the work that you do.

Whether you work in the marketplace or in ministry, as an entrepreneur or as an employee;

wherever God places you to serve, see yourself as His agent of blessing in your place of work.

Even if your current job isn't what you dream of doing in the future, be faithful during your time there. It was while David worked in the fields as a shepherd that he was being trained to one day become a king.

At every level, your work gives you the opportunity to discover more of your potential, to develop your skills and to eventually become all that God created you to be.

Prayer/Affirmation

Father, help me to see the higher purpose behind my job so that I can be an agent of blessing in my place of work.

Further study

Proverbs 19:21 (NIV)
Colossians 3:23 (AMP)

Action

Look out for ways to be a blessing at your place of work this week.

Day 20

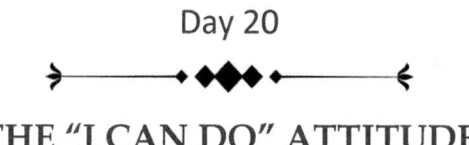

THE "I CAN DO" ATTITUDE

"I can do all things [which He has called me to do] through Him who strengthens and empowers me [to fulfill His purpose — I am self-sufficient in Christ's sufficiency; I am ready for anything and equal to anything through Him who infuses me with inner strength and confident peace.]"
—Philippians 4:13 (AMP)

The journey to success isn't always smooth. Even when God has promised you something, circumstances can try and throw you off course from your destined path. So, what do you do when obstacles stand in your way - do you shrink back in fear or do you look for a way to overcome them?

It could be that your business or job is facing trouble; or the dream in your heart hasn't yet materialized. How far you will go in life has a lot to do with your attitude when faced with such situations. A winning mentality will make all the difference.

Be like Caleb, who chose to believe even when faced with circumstances that looked contrary to what God had promised. God even commended him for having the right attitude.

> A winning mentality will make all the difference.

Don't be like the ten people who came back with a negative attitude after spotting giants in the Promised Land. There's no account that the giants even threatened them, yet those people chose to see themselves as small in comparison. Their attitude prevented them from entering into the promise.

Having an "I can do" attitude is not about having faith in your own gifts and abilities alone. Those things are blessings that you should of course be grateful for. However, your confidence and faith should be in the One Who gives you abilities and empowers you with gifts to use for His glory.

Prayer/Affirmation

I can do all the things that God has called me to do through His ability at work in me.

Further study

Numbers 14:24 (NLT)
2 Corinthians 3:5 (NIV)

Action

Think of an area of your life where you need to develop more of an "I can do" attitude.

Day 21

GET MOTIVATED

"For it is [not your strength, but it is] God who is effectively at work in you, both to will and to work [that is, strengthening, energizing, and creating in you the longing and the ability to fulfill your purpose] for His good pleasure."
—Philippians 2:13 (AMP)

From time to time, you may need a little push or nudge in the right direction. There are times when you need motivation to complete mundane everyday tasks. Other times, you will need motivation to go after your dreams.

The right kind of motivation can re-ignite a fire within your heart and move you to take the necessary action. Motivation doesn't always last very long but there are ways that you can get the daily motivation you need.

One of the major things that stop people from making measurable progress is the failure to take action. We all need a little motivation at times to help us to get going.

Perhaps there's something you've been putting off for a while, due to fear, distraction or procrastination. God can work through you to help you do the things that please Him. So, if you feel a lack of

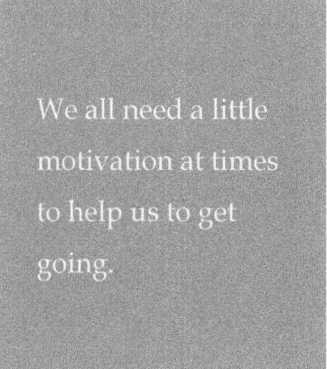

We all need a little motivation at times to help us to get going.

motivation, try spending time in prayer to fine-tune your spiritual senses to a higher frequency. When you're energized from within, that will be reflected in every other area of your life.

The Word is life-giving; therefore, meditating on at least one verse daily will help to energize you for the day ahead.

Some people have been given the gift of motivating others for the benefit of all of us. So, if you're lacking motivation, make use of these gifts by listening to or reading helpful teachings that will spur you into action.

Prayer/Affirmation

Father, energize me and help me get the motivation I need to do what I need to do today.

Further study

Proverbs 12:24 (NIV)
Hebrews 4:12 (AMP)

Action

Choose a scripture to meditate on whenever you need a little motivation today.

Day 22

THE BEST IS YET TO COME

"The path of the righteous is like the morning sun, shining ever brighter till the full light of day."
—**Proverbs 4:18 (NIV)**

We live in a world that celebrates doing things quickly and early. It's a culture that pressurizes you into doing certain things by a certain time rather than letting life unfold according to God's timing. This can lead to feelings of anxiety, inadequacy and fear of missing out.

Many people think that it's too late to fulfill their potential. They convince themselves that it's too late to further their education, too late to change their career, too late to learn something new, and too late to see the fulfillment of God's promises in their life.

However, throughout scripture, we find examples of people who saw God do great things through them much later in life. At an age when most people would have given up hope, God dramatically changed the trajectory of their lives. Moses, Abraham, Sarah and Joshua were all well advanced in age when God began to use them in extraordinary ways.

Begin to believe that the best is yet to come.

Don't let the detours and delays of life distract you from your destiny. You might be thinking that your best days are behind you but now could be the time when you step into the fullness of all that you were born to be. From today, begin to believe that the best is yet to come.

God's desire is that you continue to flourish and be fruitful through every stage of your life. It's not too late to dream, to change your career, to learn something new, to act on that idea, or to fulfill your calling.

The fact that you're still alive and reading this is a sign that you can keep growing, keep thriving and keep becoming all that God created you to be.

Prayer/Affirmation

I am alive and therefore I will continue to flourish. My future is bright and my best days are ahead of me.

Further study

Proverbs 4:18 (CEV)
2 Corinthians 3:18 (NIV)

Action

Ask God to breathe life into an old dream that you thought it was too late to achieve.

Day 23

BE A GOAL-GETTER

"Commit to the Lord whatever you do and he will establish your plans."
—Proverbs 16:3 (NLT)

Goals give you a defined focus or direction. You won't necessarily find the word "goal" mentioned often in the Bible but you will find the idea of purpose, strategy, vision and planning. All of these are essential elements for goals.

The first step towards setting and achieving a goal is to commit your plans to the Lord through prayer. He will guide you and help you achieve the right results.

Setting goals moves you closer towards invisible dreams becoming visible reality. You need to be able to "see" yourself accomplishing the goal before it actually happens. This is something that can only be done through the eyes of faith.

The motive behind your goals is also important so avoid chasing anything that is birthed out of selfish ambition. Your energy would be better spent on goals that align with God's purpose for you. The right goals will inspire you to put your faith into action and will help you maximize your potential.

> Goals give you a defined focus or direction.

Grow by Design

Finally, setting a goal and then sitting back to wait for it to happen is not much better than wishful thinking. It doesn't stop there; you need to also take action. Don't just be a goal-setter, be a goal-getter!

The accomplishment of a goal is important but ultimately what is more important is the person you will become in the process of working towards it.

Prayer/Affirmation

Father, help me to set and achieve goals that align with the right purpose and direction for my life.

Further study

Philippians 2:3 (NKJV)
1 Corinthians 9:26 (AMP)

Action

Make a brief list of action steps that you need to take to achieve your goal.

Day 24

DON'T BE LIMITED

*"Isn't this the carpenter's son?
...Where then did this man get all these things. And they took offense at him."*
—Matthew 13:55-57 (NIV)

In life, people will try and label you with their perception of who they think you are. Don't be limited by what people say about you, God created you to be so much more.

Early on in His ministry, as Jesus began to reveal more of Himself, people scoffed at him. They could not fathom that the "carpenter's son" would have the audacity to start performing miracles. Who did he think he was?!

The person you were yesterday does not necessarily determine who you will be tomorrow. In life, as you grow, develop and become more of the person that you were designed to be, there will be scoffers. There will be people who try and discourage you. They will remind you of your past, highlight your weaknesses, question your motives and reject the destiny that God has planned for you. In the end, they are only doing themselves a disservice.

> Don't be limited by what people say about you.

Don't be afraid to outgrow your past to take a hold of your future. A diamond's brilliance is determined by its many facets. God created you to shine, so go ahead and express every aspect of who He made you to be without apology. Use your gifts and follow your calling irrespective of who takes offense.

Never be limited by what small-minded people think about you. Don't let them put you in a box and label you. By the grace of God, you are who you are today and can keep becoming all you were created to be.

Prayer/Affirmation

I am expressing every part of my God-given identity and will not allow anyone to limit who I can be.

Further study

Matthew 5:16 (NIV)
Matthew 13:53- 57 (MSG)

Action

Don't be afraid to outgrow your past to take hold of your future.

Day 25

START TODAY

"If you wait for perfect conditions, you will never get anything done."
—Ecclesiastes 11:4 (TLB)

Getting started is usually the hardest part of pursuing something new. Waiting for the perfect conditions to align can often paralyze you from taking the important first steps. Common excuses include not having enough time, resources or experience. However, these are often excuses used to disguise fear and justify procrastination.

A farmer that waits for all the conditions to be perfect before sowing seed will never reap a harvest. You don't have to wait until you have everything you think you need before you can take action. If you can overcome the first hurdle of getting started, you can build momentum towards achieving your God-given dreams.

Many people have gone to the grave with dreams and ideas that they never started. They kept putting it off for another day until the days eventually ran out for them. The world has lost out on inventions, discoveries and creativity that never made it past someone's imagination.

> If you can overcome the first hurdle, you can build momentum.

Life is not a dress rehearsal, if God has placed an idea in your heart, now is the time to start doing it. Don't put your ideas on hold and don't be afraid to start small. You will learn, improve and grow along the way.

It's not too late to do the things you were supposed to do and become the person you were supposed to be. So, take a small step of faith and get started today.

Prayer/Affirmation

I refuse to put my dreams on hold any longer because the world needs me to release what God has placed inside me.

Further study

Ecclesiastes 9:10 (NIV)
Ecclesiastes 11:4 (AMP)

Action

Take a small step of faith to get started on your dream or idea today.

Day 26

DESIGNED WITH A PURPOSE

"Many are the plans in a person's heart but it's the Lord's purpose that prevails."
—Proverbs 19:21 (NIV)

God created everything with a purpose in mind, including you. You will flourish when you discover what that purpose is and walk in harmony with it. Many people struggle with the idea of finding their purpose in life but it was never supposed to be a mystery.

Your gifts and abilities could be an indicator of your purpose. A manufacturer makes a product with the right specification so that it is fit for its intended purpose. In the same way, God designed and created you so that you are fit for your own unique purpose.

Many people are using their gifts to serve the wrong things. Instead of being a blessing to the world, they become a nuisance. That is why it is so important that you use your potential to carry out God's intended purpose.

> God designed and created you for your own unique purpose.

Even the things you perceive as weaknesses or disadvantages, God can use them to bring His plans to pass in your life. It's more than likely that God is already working in you, nudging you in the direction of your destiny.

He works within you, by the Holy Spirit, causing you to have the desire to do the things that please Him. As you remain committed to walking in God's design for your life, He will continue to help you unlock more of your hidden potential.

Prayer/Affirmation

I have been created with a purpose to fulfill. God is working in me to help me do what He designed me to do.

Further study

Philippians 2:13 (AMP)
Matthew 6:24

Action

Ask God to reveal His purpose for you in this season.

Day 27

MANAGE YOUR TALENTS

> *"And to one he gave five talents, to another two, and to another one, to each according to his own ability; and immediately he went on a journey."*
> **—Matthew 25:15 (NKJV)**

The parable of the talents is one of the most well-known parables. Jesus used it to illustrate God's Kingdom; to teach us something about how it operates.

In this parable, a rich man goes away on a long journey but before he leaves, he delegates the management of his wealth to his workers by giving each of them talents to look after. A "talent," in those days, represented a sum of money.

When the rich man returned from his journey, he called the servants to each give an account of what they did with the talents he gave them. He rewarded the two who had multiplied theirs but punished the servant who buried his talent and earned nothing.

There's so much we can learn from this parable about how God expects us to manage what He gives us. This parable is an illustration of how God's Kingdom works. Therefore, the rich man represents God. The

> God expects you to properly manage what He gives you.

talent can represent something of value that God gives you to manage on His behalf.

A good investor looks for a return on their investment and God is no different. He expects you to properly manage what He gives you. You can multiply your "talents," not by neglecting them but by using them wisely.

Everyone has something of value to steward or manage for God. Talents vary from person to person but you will only be held accountable according to the measure that He gives you. So, whether you have one "talent" or five doesn't matter. If you have one talent, don't think of it as insignificant and if you have more, remember that to whom much is given much is also expected.

Prayer/Affirmation

Thank You Father for the talents that You have entrusted me with. Give me the wisdom to manage those talents well, so that they can grow and multiply.

Further study

Matthew 25:29 (AMP)
Romans 12:6-8 (NLT)

Action

Think of how you can wisely manage a "talent" that God has given to you.

Day 28

AFFIRM YOUR FAITH

"A word out of your mouth may seem of no account, but it can accomplish nearly anything – or destroy it!"
—**James 3:5 (MSG)**

Faith affirmations play a key role in your spiritual growth journey. A faith affirmation is more than just positive speaking. It's the practice of saying something that agrees with what you believe and that aligns with what God has said in His Word.

A great way to start your day is by speaking faith affirmations. It's a simple practice, yet it can make a world of difference to your mood, your mindset and the direction in which your day flows.

Learn to harness the life-giving power of words by spending a few minutes in the morning making declarations to chart the course of your day. You can do this as you get ready, while you prepare breakfast or even during your morning commute.

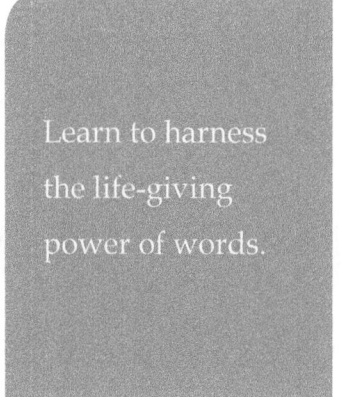

Learn to harness the life-giving power of words.

Remember that there needs to be a heart connection with the words that come out of your mouth in order for them to be most effective. The key to activating the true power of your words is to believe what you say. A faith affirmation should be an overflow of the Word that you already believe in your heart. You need to have intimate knowledge of the Word for it to settle into your heart in the first place.

Even though verbally affirming your faith is an important part of your personal growth journey, don't fall into the trap of becoming a person who merely talks. After speaking faith words, ensure that you follow through with faith actions also.

Prayer/Affirmation

I speak faith-affirming words from the overflow of my heart, that will rightly chart the course of my day.

Further study

Matthew 12:34- 35 (NLT)
2 Corinthians 4:13 (NIV)

Action

Make a list of 3 faith affirmations you can say every morning for the next 30 days.

Day 29

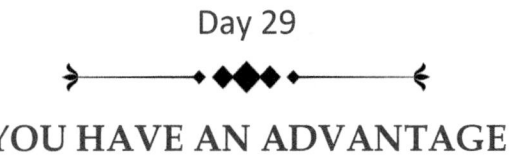

YOU HAVE AN ADVANTAGE

"It is to your advantage that I go away; for if I do not go away, the Helper will not come to you; but if I depart, I will send Him to you."
—John 16:7 (NKJV)

When Jesus left Earth, He sent us a Helper to live with us and dwell in us every day. The Helper is the Holy Spirit and without Him, you cannot become all that you were designed to be.

He was there when God created the Universe and when God put you together in your mother's womb. He knows your unique design and understands the intricacies of who you are. He sees the details of your past and shows you the possibilities of your future. He enables you to grow, mature and to become the person you were created to be.

The Holy Spirit is your personal coach, mentor and counsellor that you can access at all times. He whispers to you strategies, ideas or knowledge that you could not have figured out by yourself. He can reveal new innovations and help you produce uncommon results at work. He can guide you to make wise decisions in your

> He enables you to become the person you were created to be.

business or help you excel in your studies.

If you work in partnership with the Holy Spirit, He will cause you to produce excellence and make you stand out from the crowd. His power working in you can turn your ordinary into extraordinary and transform your natural into supernatural. You can't afford to do life without Him!

Prayer/Affirmation

Thank You Father for your Holy Spirit Who helps me, guides me and enables me in every area of my life.

Further study

John 16:7 (AMP)
1 Corinthians 12:7 (NIV)

Action

Invite the Holy Spirit to help you today.

Day 30

OVERCOMING GIANTS

"As Goliath moved closer to attack, David quickly ran out to meet him."
—1 Samuel 17:48 (NLT)

We will all face giants at some point in our lives. These may be obstacles, fears or challenges that we must overcome to get from where we are to where we need to be.

As a shepherd boy, David had to overcome a giant on his way to becoming the king that he was destined to be. There is a lot you can learn from David when faced with any giant that may stand in your way.

Firstly, what others perceived as an obstacle, David saw as an opportunity. Instead of running away from the giant, David ran towards it. When you face challenges, you can either shrink away in fear or see them as opportunities to grow to the next level.

Secondly, David was focused on winning the prize that had been promised for defeating the giant. When you face giants in your own life, remember the reason why you need to defeat them in the first place. What you focus on

> We will all face giants at some point in our lives.

becomes greater, so don't dwell on the challenge in front of you. Instead, focus on overcoming the challenge and reaching the end goal in mind.

Thirdly, David had the audacity to go into a battle carrying nothing except a slingshot and five stones. Goliath laughed at him but David was not moved. He was confident because he knew that he wasn't facing the giant alone. In spite of what he lacked, David believed that God was with him and would give him the victory.

Others saw David as a small shepherd boy but God saw him as a mighty king. In your weakness is where God is able to show up strong. So, don't be intimidated by any obstacle or challenge that stands before you. Have the audacity to boldly confront your giant and watch it fall in defeat!

Prayer/Affirmation

I am able to overcome any obstacle or challenge that stands in my way today because God is with me. I declare that any giant in my life is defeated.

Further study

1 Samuel 17:45-47 (NIV)
2 Corinthians 12:9 (NIV)

Action

Speak to the specific challenge or obstacle that you may be facing and declare your victory over it.

Day 31

GOOD SUCCESS

"For then you will make your way prosperous, and then you will have good success."
—Joshua 1:8 (NKJV)

Every one desires success in some way or another. Nobody is born with the ambition to become a failure. That is why, for generations, philosophers have written books exploring the art of success. But only God can show you the true meaning of success, through His Word.

The world often measures success in terms of material factors such as financial wealth. The problem with this standard for success is that it is based on temporary things with no eternal value. You cannot measure the true quality of a person's life by their material possessions.

God wants you to experience success in life more than you desire it for yourself. After all, what good father would not want to see their child do well? However, God desires for you to have true, lasting, good success by accomplishing His purpose for your life. Good success is not necessarily found in power, popularity, money and prestige.

> Only God can show you the true meaning of success.

A person can have these things and still fail in God's eyes.

When Joseph was a slave working in a foreign land, he would not have been considered a success by worldly standards. During that period of his life, he didn't have the wealth, possessions, influence and power that he was later blessed with. Yet, the scripture says that even in that lowly state, Joseph was successful. Joseph's story shows us that your status, wealth or possessions don't define you. True, lasting and good success is from the inside out.

Prayer/Affirmation

I am a success from the inside out, not because of the things I have but because God is with me, causing me to prevail and helping me to fulfill His purpose.

Further study

Matthew 16:26 (AMP)
Genesis 39:2 (AMP)

Action

Discover the true meaning of success through the Word of God.

Day 32

GET WISDOM

*"Wisdom is the principal thing;
Therefore get wisdom.
And in all your getting, get understanding."*
—Proverbs 4:7 (NKJV)

The Bible clearly places a high value on acquiring wisdom. After all, God gave us wonderful brains to use to think and to learn. The instruction to "get wisdom" and "get understanding" means that you must be proactive and intentional in your pursuit.

The best way to get wisdom is through God's Word. The Book of Proverbs alone is loaded with wisdom covering a broad spectrum of life issues. There are 31 chapters in the Book of Proverbs, which means there is enough daily wisdom for every month. If you want help with your business, career, finances, relationships and so on, there is wisdom to help you.

Jesus grew in wisdom so you certainly ought to do the same. The word translated, "wisdom" can also mean "the knowledge of very diverse matters." So , a great way to get wisdom and understanding is through education and reading books on a variety of useful topics.

> You must be proactive and intentional in your pursuit of wisdom.

The cost of improving your mind is small in comparison to the high price of ignorance. The right wisdom will prevent you from making costly mistakes and help you avoid unnecessary trouble in your life.

Wisdom will help you know what to do and understanding will help you know how to apply it in your life. There is no point in getting wisdom if you don't put it into practice. Don't just get wisdom, walk in wisdom also.

Prayer/Affirmation

Father, thank You for creating me with the ability to learn and understand many things. Help me to get wisdom and to understand how to apply it in my life.

Further study

Luke 2:52 (NLT)
Acts 7:22 (NLT)

Action

Read at least one Chapter of the Book of Proverbs today.

Day 33

TRAIN TO WIN

*"All athletes are disciplined in their training.
They do it to win a prize that will fade away,
but we do it for an eternal prize."*
—1 Corinthians 9:25 (NLT)

Professional athletes are super disciplined in their training. They don't just train once in a while, they train every day. Their daily routine consists of waking up early and following a strict regime in preparation for a race. An elite athlete can train for years just to compete in one Olympic Games.

Spiritual training involves engaging in activities that keep you spiritually fit. It takes patience and discipline but will help you develop the godly virtues, character and fortitude necessary to live a life of faith. Jesus was committed to spiritual training, such as praying and fasting.

In your spiritual life, you need discipline, just like an athlete. It takes dedication to cultivate the spiritual habits that will help you win the race of faith. You can't train once in a while and expect consistent results.

> In your spiritual life you need discipline.

Athletes stay focused on running their race and winning the prize. They don't focus on the crowd, they don't focus on their pain and they don't focus on their competitors.

During spiritual training, the temptation to give up will come. Keep training anyway. The path ahead of you won't necessarily be smooth; the conditions won't always be favourable; and a crowd won't always be there to cheer you on. Keep going anyway.

Remember, everyone has their own unique race to train for and to run, at their own pace. Stay focused on running your own race so that when you cross the finish line you can obtain the prize.

Prayer/Affirmation

Father, help me to get disciplined in the spiritual training I need to successfully run the race of faith.

Further study

Hebrews 12:1- 2 (NIV)
1 Timothy 4:8 (AMP)

Action

Make spiritual training a priority in your life.

Day 34

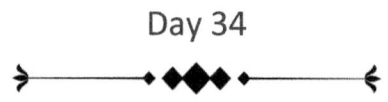

FLOURISH THROUGH STORMS

*"The righteous shall flourish like a palm tree…
They shall be fresh and flourishing."*
—Psalm 92:12,14 (NKJV)

Simple analogies about the natural world help us to understand deep spiritual truths. Palm trees are so majestic and have played an important role throughout history. There are key characteristics of a palm tree that are synonymous with God's people.

The word "flourish" means "to grow." Palm trees were designed to grow very tall. Most have the potential to reach heights of up to 70 feet tall; some can even grow as tall as 200 feet. Just like a palm tree, you are designed to flourish to your full potential.

Palm trees are well-known for being fruitful. They can produce anything from coconuts to dates, depending on their species. Even in harsh conditions, a palm tree remains fruitful.

In the same way, God created you to be fruitful. Even in harsh conditions, your life can still bear fruit, so long as you continue to trust in Him.

> You are designed to flourish to your full potential.

Palm trees are characterised by their ability to withstand the worst of storms. As the wind blows, a palm tree will bend, sometimes even touching the ground. However, when the storm ceases and the wind stops blowing, the tree will bounce right back up again. Science shows that when the trunk of a palm tree is bent by storms, it actually helps make the tree stronger. The stress of the storm causes the tree to produce a substance that toughens its internal structure.

In the same way, when the storms of life come, they cause you to produce faith that makes you stronger on the inside. Just like the palm tree, you were designed to be able to withstand difficult conditions. A tough season does not have to break you. It may require you to bend and to adapt. But it can also be an opportunity for you to toughen up and bounce back stronger than you were before.

Prayer/Affirmation

I am designed to withstand the storms of life and I am able to bounce back stronger than I was before.

Further study

Psalm 1:3 (NIV)
James 1:2-4 (NLT)

Action

Think of a "storm" you went through and how it made you stronger.

Day 35

THE RIGHT ENVIRONMENT

*"Walk with the wise and become wise,
for a companion of fools suffers harm."*
—**Proverbs 13:20 (NIV)**

Seeds must be planted in the right environment to have a good chance to grow. The right soil, enough water and plenty of light are required for seeds to flourish to their fullest. However, negative factors such as pests and weeds can prevent a seed from growing. If **you want to thrive, you** need to be in the right environment that will allow the seeds of your potential to grow.

People are the biggest influencers in our lives. That's why it is so important to be surrounded by people who will inspire, motivate or help you to become all that God created you to be. Don't spend precious time around people who demean you, discourage you or try to hold you back from pursuing your dreams.

You need people that will recognise and call out the gifts of God in you, just like the Apostle Paul did for young Timothy. He discerned Timothy's potential and encouraged him to "stir up the gift of God" within him. Paul guided and trained Timothy for

> If you want to thrive you need to be in the right environment.

ministry work, as well as gave him a good example to follow. It's fair to say that Paul played an integral role in Timothy's success in ministry.

The company you keep will help to determine how far you go in life. If you spend a lot of time with people who speak and think negatively, you will soon start doing the same. If you spend time with people who speak faith and dream big, it won't be long before you start doing the same.

Make an effort to be in the right environment that will help bring out your potential. Also, make an effort to be the type of person who adds value to those around you.

Prayer/Affirmation

Thank You Father for the people in my life who help me to grow. Lead me to be in the right environment so that the seeds You have deposited within me will flourish. Help me to also add value to the lives of those around me.

Further study

Psalm 1:1 (NIV)
Proverbs 27:17 (NIV)

Action

Thank God for one person in your life who inspires and helps you to grow.

Day 36

CHANGE THE WAY YOU THINK

"Don't copy the behavior and customs of this world, but let God transform you into a new person by changing the way you think."
—Romans 12:2 (NLT)

It can be very difficult to change a wrong mindset once it takes hold. However, the scripture above shows that it is possible to change the way you think. As you do this, you will see incredible transformation take place in your life. It may take some time but eventually, you will start to see the change happen.

The word "transformed" in the above scripture, describes a "metamorphosis," like when a caterpillar transforms into a butterfly. It means "to change from one form to another."

Renewing your mind is the equivalent of undergoing a complete renovation. When you renovate something, you make improvements to it. This usually includes repairing it, restoring it and carrying out upgrades. In the same way, when you renew your mind, this involves improving it, repairing it and upgrading to a better way of thinking.

> Old thoughts must be replaced with something better.

You cannot just simply get rid of old thoughts; they must be replaced with something better. The old, limiting thought patterns that were shaped by the world must be carefully replaced with new, Spirit-filled thoughts that are shaped by the Word of God. If you want to see your life transformed for the better, it starts by changing the way you think.

Prayer/Affirmation

My mind is being renewed by the Word of God. I am being transformed into a new person as I change the way I think.

Further study

Romans 8:6 (NIV)
Philippians 4:8 (NIV)

Action

Ask God to reveal something that you need to change about the way you think.

Day 37

THE PROCESS OF PREPARATION

"she had to complete twelve months of beauty treatments prescribed for the women, six months with oil of myrrh and six with perfumes and cosmetics."
—Esther 2:12 (NIV)

Esther had to complete twelve months of beauty treatments before she could go to see the king. It was a royal requirement for her to spend the first six months of preparation with the oil of myrrh and the last six months of preparation with perfumes and other cosmetics.

It may sound excessive but there were important hygiene reasons behind this method of preparation. The climate in the Persian Empire was very dusty and hot. Therefore, soaking in the oil of myrrh, perfumes and cosmetics purified Esther's skin, ensuring that it was clean and healthy. Her preparation was designed to bring out the best in her so that she could ultimately fulfill her destiny by saving her people.

> God will take you through a process in preparation for your destiny.

In the same way, God will take you through a process of "spiritual beautification" in preparation for your destiny. He refines you and purifies you so that you are ready to step into the fullness of your calling.

Your preparation process may look different from someone else's. It may take longer than you expected and be more tedious than you anticipated. But God designed your preparation to carefully bring out the best in you.

There is an important reason behind every step of your unique process, even if you cannot see it yet. Your preparation is the key to becoming all that God created you to be. In the end, you will find that nothing will be wasted. Everything will be used for good, to move you closer to the fulfillment of your destiny.

Prayer/Affirmation

Thank You Father, for carefully planning every step of my preparation process to refine me, to purify me and to bring out the best in me.

Further study

Esther 4:14 (NIV)
I Timothy 4:16 (AMP)

Action

Be encouraged during any period of preparation that God takes you through.

Day 38

EXPECT GOOD

*"Surely goodness and mercy shall follow me
All the days of my life.."*
—**Psalm 23:6 (NKJV)**

In the Psalm above, you can get a glimpse into the mindset of King David. He was unapologetic in declaring his expectation that the goodness of God would follow him every single day of his life. The word translated as "follow" means to "pursue" or "run after." David lived with an expectation that the goodness and unfailing love of God would prevail every day.

Some people are the opposite, they constantly expect bad things to happen to them and bad situations to follow them. As a result of a negative mindset, negative situations always seem to find them. It takes a lot of effort to expect the worse to happen all the time. Focus your energy on expecting good things instead.

When you wake up in the morning, speak good words over your day. Before you go out, declare that good things are coming your way. During the day, recognise the favor of God

> Focus your energy on expecting good things.

upon your life. Then, before you sleep, thank God for His goodness that followed you all day.

In this way, your mind will be conditioned to expect good to prevail in every circumstance. Even when bad situations come your way, keep declaring that all things will work out for your good. King David expected God's goodness, he fought many battles, yet he triumphed in each one.

Each day, you can either choose to focus more on the good, or focus on the bad. The more you celebrate God's goodness, the more His goodness will show up in your life.

Prayer/Affirmation

I expect the goodness of God to pursue me today, causing good things to come my way.

Further study

Romans 8:28 (AMP)
Philippians 4:8 (AMP)

Action

Take note of all the good things that come your way today.

Day 39

PARTNER WITH GOD

*"'I am the Lord's servant,' Mary answered.
'May your word to me be fulfilled.' Then the angel left her."*
—Luke 1:38 (NIV)

When God reveals His plans, you have to decide to partner with Him to bring those plans to pass. God has chosen you and prepared a bright future for you but He needs your participation to make it happen.

The above scripture is a powerful example of this. The young Mary was engaged to be wed, but she was willing to risk everything for the sake of answering the call of God upon her life. At the point when she said "yes" to God's plan, she didn't know how it was going to work out. She didn't know if Joseph would abandon her. She wasn't sure if her family would disown her. But she was sure of one thing – God's faithfulness in fulfilling His promise to her.

Esther had a choice, she could have continued hiding her identity and decided not to risk her life for her people. Instead, she agreed to speak to the king on their behalf. There was so much at stake but she chose to partner in God's plan for their deliverance.

> Partner with God to bring His plans to pass.

Most of the time, when God accomplishes something on the Earth, He does it through human beings. He needs you to pray, to believe, to speak up and to take action.

Perhaps God has called you to step out in faith, to take a risk or to believe for the impossible to happen. Previously you, might have made excuses like Moses; run away like Jonah; or even laughed like Sarah. God is still able and willing to fulfill His plan through you just like He did with them. He simply needs your willingness to partner with Him to carry out the fulfillment of His promises in your life.

Prayer/Affirmation

Father, I am willing to work with You to see your Word to me fulfilled in my life.

Further study

Psalm 127:1 (NIV)
Luke 1:38 (NLT)

Action

Follow through when God shows you how to partner with Him.

Day 40

DISCOVER YOUR POTENTIAL

"Since we have gifts that differ according to the grace given to us, each of us is to use them accordingly."
—**Romans 12:6 (AMP)**

Everyone has potential inside them; like hidden treasure waiting to be discovered. Potential can be described as "untapped ability" or the grace to do or become what God intended.

Archaeologists have found thousands of clay jars buried in Greece, Cyprus, Turkey and even Israel, dating back to the first century A.D. Back then, there was a common practice of placing hoards of gold coins into clay vessels and burying them in the ground for safekeeping.

From the outside, they looked like ordinary vessels but hidden inside them was a precious treasure. Some vessels remained hidden for years before their treasure was discovered, while many others will remain hidden forever.

What has God hidden inside you that is still waiting to be discovered? Perhaps you look at yourself and see an ordinary human vessel, yet inside you is a wealth of potential. There might be books waiting to be written, or

> What has God hidden inside you that is waiting to be discovered?

songs waiting to be sung. There may be a scientific breakthrough waiting to be found, or an idea waiting to be revealed.

Many people go through life never discovering the potential within them. The world desperately needs the treasure that God has hidden inside you. Let Him show you a glimpse of that potential then help you unlock and use it for His glory.

Prayer/Affirmation

Father, thank You for the potential that You have hidden inside me. Help me discover my potential and use it to do the good things which You planned for me to do.

Further study

Ephesians 2:10 (AMP)
Ephesians 4:10 (AMP)

Action

Ask God to reveal more of the potential inside you.

Day 41

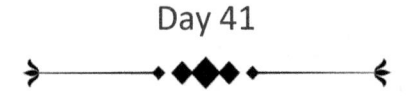

TAKE CARE OF YOUR BODY

*"For no one ever hated his own body,
but [instead] he nourishes and protects and cherishes it,
just as Christ does the church,"*
—Ephesians 5:29 (AMP)

God created and gave you your physical body, therefore, you ought to look after it carefully. Even as you focus primarily on your inner person, don't neglect your outer being also. Taking care of your body includes: eating a well-balanced, healthy diet; regular exercise; getting enough rest, and avoiding harmful acts, habits or addictions.

Moses lived to a very old age yet he remained as strong as ever. If you want your body to remain strong at every stage of life, you will have to be intentional and proactive. As much as it depends on you, make an effort to stay as healthy and fit as possible.

Appreciate your body for all that it has done and for everything it enables you to do. Your heart beats around 100,000 times a day. Every second your body produces 25 million new cells. Nobody else in the entire world has the same fingerprint

> You are fearfully and wonderfully made.

as you. You are fearfully and wonderfully made!

Your body is the temple of the Holy Spirit and the only vessel you have in which to carry out your earthly assignment. You, therefore, have a responsibility to look after it, just as you would look after the home that you live in. Although your body is temporary and won't last forever, you can use it to do great things when you take good care of it.

Prayer/Affirmation

Father, thank You for the awesome body You gave me to carry out Your purpose for me in this life. I commit to taking good care of my body and using it to glorify You.

Further study

Psalm 139:14 (NIV)
1 Corinthians 6:19-20 (NIV)

Action

Think of something you can do to take care of your body.

Day 42

STAY CONNECTED TO GOD

"Yes, I am the vine; you are the branches.
Those who remain in me, and I in them, will produce much fruit.
For apart from me you can do nothing."
—John 15:5 (NLT)

There is a lot of secular teaching about how to reach your highest potential, but a relationship with God is one essential key that should not be ignored.

For you to maximize your full potential, you must stay connected to Him. Just like fishes need water to swim and birds need the air to fly; human beings need God to function at their best.

No one can fully comprehend the depth of who you are like the One who created you. No one can fully reveal to you your capabilities like the One who designed you. No one can help you reach your full potential like the One who knows you intimately.

Without Him, you can do nothing, but through Him, you can do all things. Make it a priority to cultivate your relationship with God daily, through prayer, worship or daily study of the Word.

> Human beings need God to function at their best.

Remain connected to God so that the seed of potential in you will grow into a great harvest. In this way, you will produce good, lasting fruit that gives glory to God.

Prayer/Affirmation

I stay connected to God who is the true source of my potential. As I cultivate my relationship with Him, I am producing good, lasting fruit.

Further study

Psalm 92:13 (NIV)
John 15:4 (NLT)

Action

Think of at least one way you can cultivate a deeper relationship with God from today.

Day 43

READ YOUR MANUAL

"Your word is a lamp to guide my feet and a light for my path."
—Psalm 119:105 (NLT)

Your mobile phone has many wonderful features included in its design. However, most of these features can only be discovered if you read the device manual. The manual sets out what the product can do and how you can get the best out of it. Without it, you would probably only use the phone's basic functions without realizing that it was capable of so much more.

The Bible is your manual for living. It gives you an idea of the power you carry inside and how to use it correctly. When you read it, you will discover that there are many new capabilities inside of you waiting to be released. Don't go through life without going beyond your basic functions.

Electrical products are usually accompanied by a set of instructions. That's because electricity can be put to good use if it is properly harnessed but it can also be dangerous if it is misused.

Similarly, a person's potential can be good if it is managed correctly.

> Don't go through life without going beyond your basic functions.

Although, it can also be destructive if it is misused. If you want to be the person God designed you to be and do all the things He created you to do, don't neglect to read your manual.

Prayer/Affirmation

I am grateful for the Word of God which guides, trains and instructs me in life.

Further study

Psalm 119:105 (NIV)
2 Timothy 3:16-17 (NIV)

Action

Set aside time today to read your manual.

Day 44

EMPOWERING GRACE

"For I have worked harder than any of the other apostles; yet it was not I but God who was working through me by his grace."
—1 Corinthians 15:10 (NLT)

Grace is God's "unmerited favor" working in your life. Grace is also God's divine influence working on the inside of a person, which manifests on the outside.

It can be frustrating to receive a gift that requires batteries when the batteries are not included. You cannot use something if it doesn't have the power it requires to make it work. Grace is like the battery that empowers the gifts of God. Thankfully, God doesn't give us such gifts without including the power required to make them work. He always supplies the grace to put His various gifts to good use.

Grace enables you to work in a manner that is pleasing to God. The Apostle Paul made it clear, in the opening scripture, that he excelled because of God's grace working through him.

The particular grace you have will be dormant and ineffective unless you actually put your gifts to work. If you are creative, then use your creativity to serve. If you have the gift of teaching, then

> Grace is like the battery that empowers the gifts of God.

teach to bless others. If you have the gift of giving, then give generously to people in need. You don't need to wait for permission or approval from anyone else to operate in the grace that you have already been given.

Prayer/Affirmation

Thank You Father for Your grace, which empowers me to use Your gifts, in the way that You intended.

Further study

Romans 12:6-8 (NIV)
1 Peter 4:10 (NIV)

Action

Once you have identified the particular grace that you have been given, go ahead and put it to work.

Day 45

GROW UP IN ALL THINGS

"...let us grow up in all things into Him [following His example] who is the Head – Christ..."
—Ephesians 4:15 (AMP)

There are people who are spiritually sound, but lack the wisdom to manage the affairs of life. Some are intellectually brilliant, but incapable of relating with other people. Then some people are physically fit, but spiritually unhealthy. No loving parent would want to see their child's growth and development hindered in any way. God's desire for you as His child, is that you thrive in all areas, as you grow up in Christ.

The Bible tells us that Jesus grew in four distinct ways. He grew "in wisdom," which means that He grew on an intellectual level. He grew "in stature," which means that He grew on a physical level. He grew "in favor with God" which implies that He grew on a spiritual level. Finally, He grew "in favor with all the people," which implies that He grew on a relational level.

> Don't neglect any area of your development.

Jesus gave the best example of all-round personal growth which you can also follow. Don't neglect any area of your development if you want to truly function at your best.

Prayer/Affirmation

I am growing up in all things and will not neglect any area of my personal development.

Further study

Luke 2:52 (NLT)
James 1:4 (NIV)

Action

Look for ways to grow in any area of your development that you may have neglected.

Day 46

THE KEY TO BEING GREAT

"Instead, whoever wants to become great among you must be your servant…"
—**Matthew 20:26 (NIV)**

There is nothing wrong with aspiring for greatness, so long as you're driven by the right motivation. In the above scripture, Jesus gave us a powerful key to measure true greatness.

Greatness isn't necessarily measured by how many titles you have, or how many people you exercise authority over. People become great at the service of others not at the expense of others.

You can serve by using your gifts to do something for someone. This is how God measures greatness. Every day brings a new opportunity to be great. The more you invest in your service to others, the greater you will become.

> Every day brings a new opportunity to be great.

If you want to be a great employee, faithfully serve the company or organisation that you work for. If you want to be a great leader, look for ways to serve the people you lead. If you want to run a great business, think of ways to provide excellent customer service.

There are some levels of influence that you will never reach until you begin to serve. No matter who you are, what you do or where you come from, you can become great when you learn this principle.

If you want to be great, follow the example of the greatest man who ever lived; His focus was not to be served but to serve others.

Prayer/Affirmation

Father, help me to see that true greatness comes from serving others. Help me to look for ways to serve and add value to people's lives.

Further study

Matthew 20:26 (NIV)
Matthew 23:12 (NIV)

Action

Look for ways to serve at church, through your work, in your neighborhood or at home.

Day 47

GUARD YOUR HEART

*"Guard your heart above all else,
for it determines the course of your life."*
—Proverbs 4:23 (NLT)

Some people think that they have no control or influence over the things that happen in their lives. They go through life with the attitude of "what will be will be." In fact, you do have a lot of influence over the direction of your life because your outer world is largely determined by your inner world.

Your outer world is your external reality. Your inner world is your "heart" and who you are on the inside. Your heart is the invisible control centre of your life that is made up of your thoughts and beliefs. That is why the Book of Proverbs instructs you to carefully guard your heart.

You "guard" your heart like a security guard would watch over the entry point of a building. Whatever enters through the entry point of your mind, has the chance to settle in your heart and eventually determine the direction in which your life goes.

> Your heart is the invisible control centre of your life.

If you're full of unbelief, doubt and thoughts that are contrary to God's Word, then those things will be able to influence the direction of your life.

Make an effort to actively store up the Word of God and good thoughts in your heart, so that the right things can influence your life in the right direction.

Prayer/Affirmation

Father, show me how to carefully guard my heart so that my life heads in the right direction.

Further study

Proverbs 4:23 (NIV)
Matthew 12:35 (NLT)

Action

Make an effort to watch over the things you allow into your mind.

Day 48

LOVE IS THE KEY

"If I had the gift of prophecy, and if I understood all of God's secret plans and possessed all knowledge, and if I had such faith that I could move mountains, but didn't love others, I would be nothing."
—**1 Corinthians 13:2 (NLT)**

There is no point in doing all the most amazing things in the world with your God-given talents and gifts if you are not motivated by love for others. These things amount to nothing unless you walk in love.

It's interesting how right in the middle of his teaching on spiritual gifts in 1 Corinthians ch 12 and 14, Paul suddenly shifts and starts teaching on love in chapter 13. It's almost as though he takes a brief detour. However, he's drawing the reader's attention to the fact that love must be central when using your gifts.

Too many times, you hear stories of people who were blessed with extraordinary talent but ended up harming themselves or others. If you want to produce good fruit, your roots must be grounded in love.

> Your roots must be grounded in love.

Love is the key to using your potential in the way that God intended. Unlike selfishness, love will stop you from destroying yourself or others. It's good to cultivate your gifts but remember to follow the way of love when doing so.

Prayer/Affirmation

Father, show me if there are any areas where I have been selfish and help me to follow the way of love in all that I do.

Further study

1 Corinthians 14:1 (NIV)
Philippians 2:3- 4 (NIV)

Action

Let love be your motivation.

Day 49

SEE THE BIGGER PICTURE

*"That person is like a tree planted by streams of water,
which yields its fruit in season
and whose leaf does not wither —
whatever they do prospers."*
—Psalm 1:3 (NIV)

In nature, trees provide shelter, oxygen and nourishment, which enables the world around them to thrive. The ecosystem as a whole benefits when each individual tree grows to its potential. As a tree flourishes, the world around it flourishes too. Similarly, you are part of a bigger picture. The benefits of you maximizing your potential extend beyond yourself. The more you flourish, the more the world around you will also flourish.

Christ is described as the vine and believers are the branches. For the Church as a whole to grow to maturity, all the individual members, or branches, should be growing and functioning in their purpose. All of the individual members of a vine are interconnected.

> The more you flourish, the more the world around you will also flourish.

The Church is the body of Christ. For the body to function healthily as a whole, each member must be functioning properly according to their design. The legs function when the knees work in the way that they are supposed to. The arms function when the elbows are working properly.

Every part of the body relies on another. If one part suffers, then the whole body suffers. So, don't see yourself as insignificant, you are an important part of a much bigger picture. Your impact and influence extend far beyond what you imagine or think.

Prayer/Affirmation

I am an important and vital member of the wider body of Christ.

Further study

John 15:2 (NLT)
1 Corinthians 12:21-26 (NIV)

Action

Think of the important role you play in your family, neighborhood, or community.

Day 50

EMBRACE THE NEW

*"He prunes the branches that do bear fruit
so they will produce even more.."*
—John 15:2 (NLT)

Sometimes you go through seasons of pruning in order to grow and develop to your full potential. Pruning gets rid of the old, dead things in your life. It's the process of removing things that have been hindering you from moving forward in your purpose, thereby allowing you to grow and be fruitful. Pruning can be painful, but it is necessary for growth.

The primary sign of a season of pruning is the suffering of loss. This can stir up feelings of discouragement or disappointment as you may question if you have done something wrong. But remember, it is only the fruitful branches that are pruned. It could be a sign that you are doing well, and that God wants to encourage your growth further.

When you look around and it seems that things are falling apart, perhaps, it could actually be the start of something new emerging. God wants to take you beyond the limitations of your past so that you can embrace the new opportunities that lie ahead. New gifts, new grace and new

> Embrace the new opportunities that lie ahead.

ideas will be released to enable you to walk in all that He has prepared for you.

It may seem daunting at first. However, if you stay attached to the old, whether mentally, emotionally, physically or spiritually - you will neglect to take hold of the new. The future ahead of you can be greater than your past. Be bold and let go of the old, embrace the new and step into all that God is leading you into.

Prayer/Affirmation

I let go of the old things that God wants to prune from my life and embrace the new, bright future He is leading me to.

Further study

Isaiah 43:18-19 (NLT)
John 12:24 (NIV)

Action

Let go of the old things that God is removing and prepare to embrace the new.

Day 51

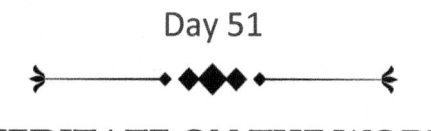

MEDITATE ON THE WORD

"This Book of the Law shall not depart from your mouth, but you shall meditate in it day and night... For then you will make your way prosperous, and then you will have good success."
—Joshua 1:8 NKJV

God instructed Joshua to meditate on God's teachings and directions (Book of the Law) so that he would be successful in his mission of leading the people into the Promised Land. This is echoed in Psalm 1, which tells us that the person who meditates on God's teachings and directions (law) will prosper in all they do.

God's Word is both living and active; meaning it's alive and it's life-giving. It has the power to transform your heart, renew your mind and improve your life.

The word translated as "meditate" means to ponder, to study or even to speak. All of these actions are a form of meditation. Biblical meditation doesn't focus on yourself or your own thoughts. Instead, it focuses on God's teachings and directions, as expressed through His Word.

> Whatever you focus on will have the greatest influence.

Whatever you focus on the most will have the greatest influence on you, so be careful not to unintentionally meditate on the wrong things. As you ponder, study or speak God's Word, you are able to activate its power and influence over your life.

Every day, you can choose a scripture that relates to your current season of life to meditate on. It will influence you to walk in wisdom and lead you on the path of true success.

Prayer/Affirmation

Father, thank You for Your Word which has the power to transform my heart, renew my mind and improve my life as I meditate on it today.

Further study

Psalm 1:2-3 (AMP)
Hebrews 4:12 (NIV)

Action

Spend a few minutes meditating on a life-giving scripture today.

Day 52

SEE TREASURE IN OTHERS

"Isn't this the carpenter's son? Isn't his mother's name Mary, and aren't his brothers James, Joseph, Simon and Judas?"
Matthew 13:55 (NIV)

People have the tendency to judge others based on their outward appearance alone. If only you could see the extraordinary treasure hidden inside ordinary people that you meet every day, you may have a different opinion about them.

Who would have thought that a little shepherd boy would become a mighty king? People overlooked him but God chose David as the vessel to carry his anointing. Who would have imagined that the Jewish orphan would become Queen of Persia? Yet, God chose Esther and positioned her in the palace to help save her people.

The people in Jesus' hometown could not comprehend who He really was. To them, He was simply "the carpenter's son" but truly, He was the Saviour of the world. They missed out on the blessing that He carried because they couldn't recognise the anointing. The One they disregarded, was the One sent by God to save them.

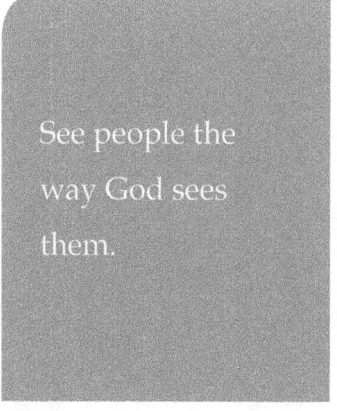

See people the way God sees them.

Be the type of person who sees people the way God sees them and recognise the treasure in others. The more you appreciate the gifts that other people carry, the more you will be blessed by them.

Prayer/Affirmation

Father, open my eyes to see people like You do and to recognise the true treasure in others.

Further study

John 1:10- 12 (NIV)
2 Corinthians 4:7 (NIV)

Action

Look beyond outward appearance and you will see the blessing that other people carry.

Day 53

SHOW YOURSELF GRACE

"My grace is sufficient for you, for my power is made perfect in weakness."
—2 Corinthians 12:9 (NIV)

Sometimes people carry the burden of past hurts, failures and mistakes in the form of bitterness, regret and self-condemnation. Don't be hard on yourself when things go wrong. God doesn't expect you to rely on your own strength; His grace is enough for you.

When you are weak, that is when God's strength is able to work through you. So, as you show grace towards other people, don't forget to show grace to yourself also.

You can start by showing yourself grace through your thoughts. Forgive yourself for any past mistakes and move on with the determination to do better now that you know better. Be grateful for how far you have come and see every experience as an opportunity to grow.

You can show grace to yourself through your words. The words you speak over yourself are important. Don't belittle, ridicule or speak harshly about yourself. Words have creative power and

> God's grace is enough for you.

determine the course of your life. Show yourself grace by speaking kind words over yourself.

You can also show grace to yourself through your actions. Don't apply unnecessary pressure or set unreasonable expectations for yourself. Instead, allow yourself to flow in the grace of God which will take you further than you could ever go in your own strength.

Prayer/Affirmation

Father, I receive Your grace which is enough for me today. I do not rely on my own strength because I know that You strengthen me in all of my weaknesses.

Further study

Matthew 11:28-30 (MSG)
2 Corinthians 12:9-10 (NIV)

Action

Speak kind and gracious words over yourself today.

Day 54

BE FRUITFUL

"You didn't choose me. I chose you. I appointed you to go and produce lasting fruit..."
John 15:16 (NLT)

There was an incident when Jesus was hungry and came across a fig tree upon which He expected to find fruit. It was not yet the season for figs to appear, however, this particular tree caught His attention because it was already displaying leaves. Fig trees are not supposed to show leaves unless they are accompanied by fruit. It was therefore reasonable for Jesus to expect that this tree should also have fruit.

Instead, He found nothing, so He cursed the tree and by the next day, it had withered from its roots.

God expects you to produce real, lasting fruit. He doesn't want you to put on a show with no substance. There are people who are more concerned with the way they appear on the outside than developing their character on the inside. The Pharisees were this way and Jesus called them out for such behaviour.

Grow by Design

When God examines your life, what will He see – real spiritual fruit, or an empty external display? The main cause of fig trees not producing fruit is lack of maturity. Don't fall into the trap of appearing godly, talking religious or acting righteous without growing in spiritual maturity and having a real relationship with God.

Prayer/Affirmation

Father, help me to cultivate real, lasting fruit by growing in spiritual maturity and in my relationship with You.

Further study

Matthew 23:5-7 (NLT)
Mark 11:12-13 (NIV)

Action

Focus on growing in spiritual maturity so that you can be fruitful.

Day 55

WORK ON YOUR PERSONAL DEVELOPMENT

"Pay close attention to yourself [concentrate on your personal development] and to your teaching.."
—1 Timothy 4:16 (AMP)

Personal development is the process of intentionally developing and improving yourself. Reading books, undergoing training and completing courses are activities which help personal development, alongside studying God's Word.

In his letter to Timothy, Paul instructed him to pay as much attention to his personal development as he did to his teaching. Paul knew that, for Timothy to become the well-rounded minister that God had called him to be, he had to work on himself.

Like Timothy, you will need to work on the aspects of your personal development necessary to fulfill your purpose or calling. The areas of personal development that need the most focus will differ from person to person, but everyone needs to

> Everyone needs to work on themselves in some way.

work on themselves in some way.

Do something every day that will help your personal development. Focus on developing the right kind of mindset, skills, knowledge, habits and character.

Even though some effort is required on your part, you don't have to do it in your own strength. The Holy Spirit will help you during every step of your personal development journey and make your efforts successful.

Prayer/Affirmation

I commit to working on my personal development with the help of the Holy Spirit.

Further study

Psalms 90:17 (NLT)
1 Timothy 4:15-16 (AMP)

Action

Work on your personal development today.

Day 56

OVERCOME FEAR

"And I was afraid, and went and hid your talent in the ground."
—**Matthew 25:25 (NKJV)**

Fear can hold you back from becoming all that God created you to be and doing all that He has called you to do. Fear can show up in many ways. There's the fear of failure, fear of the unknown, fear of rejection, fear of what others might think and so on. Fear causes delays, excuses and even discouragement.

Most times, the thing you fear could be the very thing that God is calling you to do. In the Parable of the Talents, the servant who buried his talent did so because he was afraid.

Before going on his journey, the rich man had given each of his servants clear instructions about what to do with their talents. The servant to whom he gave one talent didn't follow the instruction; instead, he allowed fear to control his actions.

When God asks you to give an account of the "talent" that He gave you, will you say you were afraid to do what He asked you to do with it? If you want to fulfill God's purpose, you need to overcome fear.

> The thing you fear could be the very thing that God is calling you to do.

Many people bury ideas, dreams and callings because they are afraid. Don't allow fear to hold you back from your destiny. Every time you make a choice to step out in faith and take action in spite of any fear that you feel, that fear will shrink until it no longer has any influence over you.

Prayer/Affirmation

I will not allow fear to stop me from walking in the fullness of my destiny. With God's help, I can overcome fear and do all the things that He has called me to do.

Further study

2 Timothy 1:7 (NKJV)
Isaiah 41:13 (NIV)

Action

Take a step of faith to overcome fear today.

Day 57

BE FILLED WITH THE SPIRIT

"Don't be drunk with wine, because that will ruin your life. Instead, be filled with the Holy Spirit..."
—Ephesians 5:18 (NLT)

If you want to maximize your potential, you cannot neglect the ministry of the Holy Spirit in your life. The opening scripture instructs us to be filled with the Holy Spirit. This is not supposed to be a one-time occurrence; you must be continually filled with the Holy Spirit.

Jesus was filled with the Holy Spirit before He began His earthly ministry. If Jesus needed to be filled with the Holy Spirit to carry out His purpose, then so do we.

The apostles were filled with the Holy Spirit to enable them to carry out their ministries. Most notably, after Peter was filled with the Holy Spirit, he was dramatically transformed. He went from being the disciple who was afraid and had denied Jesus, to becoming a bold, fearless apostle.

The Holy Spirit gives you the boldness and power to do the things that you are called to do, in the way that you were designed to do them. If you want to maximize

> You must be continually filled with the Holy Spirit.

your God-given potential, you must be regularly filled with the Holy Spirit.

Prayer/Affirmation

Father, may I be continually filled with Your Holy Spirit and may Your power work through me, helping me to do the things You have called me to do.

Further study

Acts 1:8 (NIV)
Luke 4:1 (NIV)

Action

Ask the Holy Spirit to fill you today.

Day 58

HAVE AN ATTITUDE OF GRATITUDE

"...give thanks in all circumstances; for this is God's will for you in Christ Jesus."
—1 Thessalonians 5:18 (NIV)

It's easy to be grateful when things are going well but it is important to keep an attitude of gratitude even through difficult times. There is always something for you to be thankful for.

Make it a habit to look out for the good in any situation and take notice of even the smallest blessings. As you do this, more and more reasons to be grateful will show up in your life.

Don't take blessings such as good health and a home to live in for granted. Also, avoid the trap of comparing yourself with other people, as this will make you despise the value of your own blessings.

Research shows that having a grateful attitude can increase your motivation and productivity levels, therefore helping you to achieve your goals.

> There is always something for you to be thankful for.

Counting your blessings is a powerful way to overcome worry, discouragement and disappointment. When you practice this regularly, it will help you improve your mindset, change your perspective and inject fresh enthusiasm into your life.

Being grateful for past victories will help you realize how much progress you are really making. No matter how far you still have to go, always be grateful for how far you have already come.

Prayer/Affirmation

I choose to have an attitude of gratitude today and I am thankful to God for all of the blessings in my life.

Further study

Psalm 107:1 (NLT)
Philippians 4:6-7 (NIV)

Action

Write down at least 3 things that you are grateful for today.

Day 59

POSITIONED FOR SUCCESS

"They love the Lord's teachings, and they think about those teachings day and night. They are strong, like a tree planted by a river. The tree produces fruit in season, and its leaves don't die. Everything they do will succeed."
—Psalm 1:2-3 (NCV)

If you want to excel in any area of life, you must be positioned for success. The opening scripture uses the analogy of a healthy tree growing to its full potential. The tree doesn't struggle to grow, to produce leaves or to bear fruit. It thrives naturally because it is positioned in the right place. The constant supply of nourishment from the river provides the right conditions for the tree to grow strong, be fruitful and remain evergreen.

In a similar way, constant nourishment by the Word of God will position you for success in everything you do. It will enable you to grow strong, be fruitful and remain evergreen.

The Word of God is the constant supply you need to grow to your full potential. As the tree planted by the river doesn't struggle to grow; a person that is well-watered by the Word of God doesn't have to struggle to be successful. It will shape your

> If you want to excel in any area of life, you must be positioned for success.

thoughts, influence your decisions and guide your actions. It will cause you to think the right way, make the right choices and take the right steps, even without you knowing it.

Prayer/Affirmation

Father, thank You for your Word that nourishes me and enables me to grow to my full potential.

Further study

Jeremiah 17:7- 8 (AMP)
Acts 20:32 (MSG)

Action

Position yourself for success by reflecting on the Word of God throughout the day.

Day 60

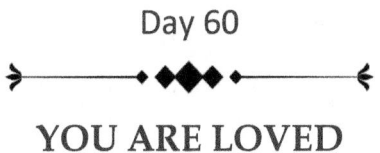

YOU ARE LOVED

"And may you have the power to understand, as all God's people should, how wide, how long, how high, and how deep his love is."
—Ephesians 3:18 (NLT)

God is a good Father who wants the best for you. He wants you to succeed in life and to be everything that He designed you to be. A major reason why people don't do well in life is that they don't believe that God wants them to do well.

A lot of people don't expect good things because they don't believe God wants to be good to them. However, a personal revelation of God's love will transform your life for the better.

Every good thing given to you comes from God. He didn't create you to be a failure, to lack or to suffer. His plans for you are good, to give you a bright future.

To walk in the fullness of your God-given destiny, you must have an understanding of the multi-dimensional nature of His love towards you. It's not enough to read about it, you need to experience this love for yourself.

A fresh revelation of God's love will help you have a more positive outlook, even when

> A personal revelation of God's love will transform your life for the better.

difficult times come. It will give you the richest experience of God in every area of your life.

When you understand the extent of the Father's love towards you, you will be compelled to make the most of the gifts, talents and time that He has given you. You will walk by faith instead of being intimidated by fear. You will expect the best instead of assuming the worse. You will not settle for less than all that God has planned for you.

Prayer/Affirmation

Father, give me a fresh and personal revelation of the extent of your love towards me.

Further study

Ephesians 3:18-19 (AMP)
1 John 4:18 (NIV)

Action

Spend a few minutes today reflecting on God's love for you.

Bible Reference

Scriptures marked AMP are taken from the AMPLIFIED BIBLE (AMP): Scripture taken from the AMPLIFIED® BIBLE, Copyright © 2015 by The Lockman Foundation, La Habra, CA 90631. All rights reserved.

Scripture taken from THE HOLY BIBLE, NEW INTERNATIONAL VERSION ®. Copyright© 1973, 1978, 1984, 2011 by Biblica, Inc.™. Used by permission of Zondervan

Scriptures marked CEV are taken from the CONTEMPORARY ENGLISH VERSION (CEV): Scripture taken from the CONTEMPORARY ENGLISH VERSION copyright© 1995 by the American Bible Society. Used by permission.

Scriptures marked NLT are taken from the HOLY BIBLE, NEW LIVING TRANSLATION (NLT): Scriptures taken from the HOLY BIBLE, NEW LIVING TRANSLATION, Copyright© 1996, 2004, 2007 by Tyndale House Foundation. Used by permission of Tyndale House Publishers, Inc., Carol Stream, Illinois 60188. All rights reserved. Used by permission.

Scriptures marked KJV are taken from the KING JAMES VERSION (KJV): KING JAMES VERSION, public domain.

Scriptures marked ESV are taken from the THE HOLY BIBLE, ENGLISH STANDARD VERSION (ESV): Scriptures taken from THE HOLY BIBLE, ENGLISH STANDARD VERSION ® Copyright© 2001 by Crossway, a publishing ministry of Good News Publishers. Used by permission.

Scriptures marked TLB are taken from the THE LIVING BIBLE (TLB): Scripture taken from THE LIVING BIBLE copyright© 1971. Used by permission of Tyndale House Publishers, Inc., Carol Stream, Illinois 60188. All rights reserved.

Scriptures marked NKJV are taken from the NEW KING JAMES VERSION (NKJV): Scripture taken from the NEW KING JAMES VERSION®. Copyright© 1982 by Thomas Nelson, Inc. Used by permission. All rights reserved.

Scripture quotations marked MSG are taken from *THE MESSAGE*, copyright © 1993, 2002, 2018 by Eugene H. Peterson. Used by permission of NavPress. All rights reserved. Represented by Tyndale House Publishers, Inc.

Scriptures marked NCV are taken from the NEW CENTURY VERSION (NCV): Scripture taken from the NEW CENTURY VERSION®. Copyright© 2005 by Thomas Nelson, Inc. Used by permission. All rights reserved.

For further resources, or more details about this book or the author, please
visit www.GrowByDesignBook.com

About Kharis Publishing

Kharis Publishing, an imprint of Kharis Media LLC, is a leading Christian and inspirational book publisher based in Aurora, Chicago metropolitan area, Illinois. Kharis' dual mission is to give voice to under-represented writers (including women and first-time authors) and equip orphans in developing countries with literacy tools. That is why, for each book sold, the publisher channels some of the proceeds into providing books and computers for orphanages in developing countries so that these kids may learn to read, dream, and grow. For a limited time, Kharis Publishing is accepting unsolicited queries for nonfiction (Christian, self-help, memoirs, business, health and wellness) from qualified leaders, professionals, pastors, and ministers. Learn more at: About Us - Kharis Publishing - Accepting Manuscript

www.ingramcontent.com/pod-product-compliance
Lightning Source LLC
LaVergne TN
LVHW051524070426
835507LV00023B/3289